A Child's Book of Early Church History

Path of Truth

Written and Illustrated by
Amy Schlabach

ISBN 10: 193375326-9
ISBN 13: 978-193375326-3

Written and illustrated by Amy Schlabach
Book design by Rosetta Mullet

Carlisle Press
WALNUT CREEK
2673 TR 421
Sugarcreek, OH 44681
800.852.4482

SWITZERLAND

ASIA MINOR

ITALY

ROME

PHILIPPI

THESSALONICA

BEREA

ATHENS

MALTA

CRETE

CYPRUS

DAMASCUS

JERUSALEM

MEDITERRANEAN SEA

Lands of the early Christians

The empty tomb of Jesus

An Ancient Faith

At the empty tomb of Jesus the angels told His disciples that Jesus was risen! After Jesus was crucified, His followers wondered if maybe He wasn't the Son of God after all. Now they heard what the angels said and hope rose in their hearts. Could it be true? The news traveled quickly, and hundreds gathered to listen to all the things Jesus told them before He went back to heaven. This gave them courage to be faithful even though Jewish and Roman leaders tortured them in horrible ways. As the first Christian church grew and spread from place to place, the persecution followed close behind.

For hundreds of years Christians were persecuted. They were burned alive and fed to lions in the arenas of the Roman Empire. The Romans tortured them in every evil way they could think of. But more and more people believed in Jesus. The followers of Jesus were turning the world upside down with His teachings!

Then one night the Roman Emperor Constantine dreamed about Jesus. He thought Jesus told him to go into battle the next day, using a cross as a good-luck symbol. He won the battle. After that he made laws that protected Christians. He did many good things for them.

But Constantine did not really understand what God's kingdom was about. He gave Christians homes and money. They were sad and tired from the vicious tortures they had gone through, and Constantine's gifts seemed like an answer to prayer.

Early Christians were thrown to the lions in the arenas of Rome

Most of the Christians in the Roman Empire thought Constantine was a blessing to the believers. They had lived in poverty and fear, hiding from the authorities and being tormented for hundreds of years. Being treated so well by the Emperor felt wonderful. He gave the Christians powerful jobs in his court, and had churches built for them that were as big and grand as the temples of the Roman gods. But some of the Christians did not like these changes.

Roman Christians talk about the changes made by Constantine

The Roman emperor Constantine gave riches and power to the Christians

Constantine now wanted to be the leader of the church and punished people who did not agree with him. Instead of loving his enemies, he killed anyone who was a danger to his throne, even his own son Crispus.

The Christians thought the Empire would be filled with peace and happiness now that they were a part of it, but they were sadly mistaken. Jesus had told His followers that His kingdom was not of this world, and by being led astray the Christians lost a great blessing.

After the Christians were deceived by Constantine's dream, it was only fourteen years until some of them turned their backs on Jesus' teachings of love and peace. They started punishing others who disagreed with them. Many of those they persecuted were true Christians who wanted a pure church.

The German warriors destroy Rome.

Many Romans joined a Christian church because they found out that the Emperor would favor them. But, like Constantine, their hearts were not changed. They saw Christianity as just another way to get more for themselves. The new converts brought many evil things, like idol worship, into the church.

Rome kept getting weaker and weaker. Many people called themselves followers of Jesus. By the time the Roman Empire fell, this false kind of Christianity had spread throughout the German tribes that conquered them. So people who called themselves Christians were now killing each other in war. It was the complete opposite of what Jesus taught. How sad He must have been to see how those who called themselves His followers didn't live the way He taught. Still, throughout the Middle Ages there were people who wanted to love and obey Jesus. They kept their lights shining brightly for Him!

The Poor in Spirit

During the Middle Ages in the busy city of Lyons, France, there lived a man named Waldes. He was a merchant and had a great fleet of ships. The ships sailed to faraway ports and brought back things like gold, ivory, and exotic spices. Waldes was a very rich man, but he was not happy.

One day, as he talked with the leaders of the city one of them suddenly collapsed and died. Waldes was terrified when he thought back over his life. He wondered what would happen if he were to die. He began to search eagerly for God's will. Going to the local priest, Waldes told him how he wanted more for his life than just making money and spending it. The priest showed him the story of the rich young man in Matthew nineteen. Waldes was touched when he heard that Jesus told the young man to sell all he had, and he would have treasure in heaven. Then Jesus told the man to come and follow Him.

Waldes was a rich merchant who sold everything he had to follow Jesus.

Waldes felt these words were meant just for him. He decided to make changes in his life and do what Jesus wanted. He sold the things he owned and used some of the money to have Bibles translated and printed in the local language.

Then Waldes gave the rest of his money to the poor people in the city. His wealthy friends thought he was going crazy. He tried to tell them that he wasn't crazy, he was just doing what God wanted him to do! He was tired of worrying about his money and being tied down by his riches. So Waldes gave away his money and began sharing the joy he had found with everyone he met.

The people were so eager for the Word of God that soon he was teaching a large group of people in his house. They called themselves the Poor in Spirit, and before long the whole city talked about the bold men preaching in the streets and markets. When the local Catholic Bishop heard about this, he warned Waldes and the others to quit preaching. He did not mind their new way of living. He liked the help they gave to the poor. But the Roman Church said that preaching may only be done by those trained at their universities and ordained by the Church.

The Catholic Bishop in Lyons warns Waldes
to leave the preaching to the priests

Waldes told him that preaching and teaching should be done by all men who followed the Apostles' example. This made the Bishop angry and in the next few years he warned them over and over to keep quiet. The Poor in Spirit did not listen to him. Finally he excommunicated them from the Church.

Still the group kept growing and the leaders kept preaching their sermons, so the authorities had them banished from Lyons. The Poor in Spirit rejoiced to be persecuted for Jesus' sake! They traveled all over Europe telling people about their faith.

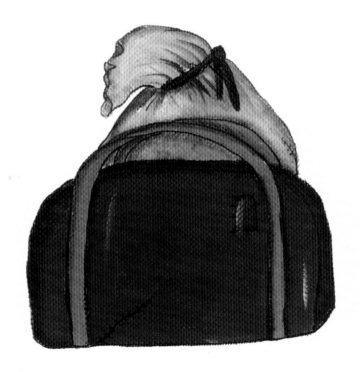

The Poor in Spirit leave Lyons with only what they could carry

Many other small groups of true Christians joined them in spreading their message of denying self and living for Christ. Some of these people spoke against traditions the Roman Catholics had added to the Scriptures. After carefully studying the Bible, Waldes and the Poor in Spirit saw that they were right, and also began to tell the people that many of the things the priests said were holy were only their ideas and not the true teachings of Jesus. Because of this the Catholics called them heretics and hunted them down. They killed and tortured them. For the next three hundred years these people suffered for their faith. Most of the Waldensians, as they were now called, were killed, but small groups survived.

Sometimes the Pope sent his soldiers, called Crusaders, to kill whole villages of Waldensians. Men, women, and children were massacred by soldiers who said they were doing the work of the Lord!

The Crusaders attack a Waldensian village late at night

Now the Waldensians that were left in Italy heard about the Reformation going on in Germany and Switzerland. They were excited and sent a few of their leaders to find out more about it. Traveling over the Alps from Italy to Switzerland, these men met a friend of Ulrich Zwingli, one of the leaders of the Reformation. He was very happy to meet the Waldensians. These people had survived alone against the mighty Roman Church for hundreds of years! He told them all about the Reformation and invited them to be a part of it.

When they got back home, the Waldensian leaders talked about what they had learned. Some of them knew right away that the Reformers were missing some of the most important teachings of Jesus and wanted nothing more to do with them. Others were excited and flattered by the invitation and wanted to join the Reformers right away.

They talked it over for several years and by then most had changed their minds. They joined the Reformation, but by doing this they lost most of the true faith that the Poor in Spirit had struggled to live by. Later a few of the Waldensians joined the Anabaptists, but the others, as part of the newly reformed church, were soon persecuting people in the same way they once had been. By changing their beliefs to fit in with their new friends, most of the Waldensians ended up losing the things that had set them apart for hundreds of years.

Anabaptism Is Born

In the shadow of the mighty Swiss Alps, the winds of change swirled across the countryside. The sleepy little towns and villages were caught up in unrest and excitement as the Reformation swept across Europe.

For hundreds of years the Catholic Church insisted that it wasn't safe for anyone but the priests to read the Bible. They thought that if common, everyday people read the Bible, they would not understand it. But the leaders of the Reformation were having Bibles printed that anyone could buy! The Bibles cost a lot, but many people had longed for one all their lives. It was wonderful to be able to read God's Word for themselves instead of just hearing priests read the Latin Bible that had been used for hundreds of years. Most of the common people did not understand Latin very well.

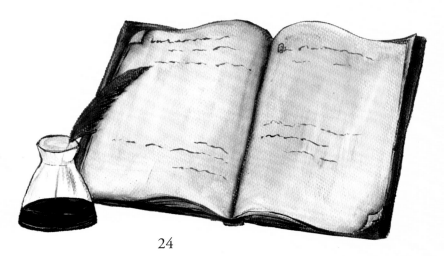

Ulrich Zwingli and his friends talk about the Bible and what it teaches

Ulrich Zwingli, one of the leading Reformers, was a well educated priest. He had been the head of a large church in Zurich, Switzerland. He won over the authorities with his preaching, and they helped him in his goal to change the people of Switzerland.

He tried to force everyone to go to the new churches, and since he was a talented speaker, many people listened to him. But several of Ulrich's friends began to see that the Reformation was missing parts of the true Gospel of Jesus. These friends studied the Bible and tried to show Ulrich what they found. They told Ulrich that it wasn't right to use force to make people go to church. These men said that a Christian's whole life needs to be separated from the world. They insisted that the teachings of Jesus must be followed in their everyday lives.

So much of the people's religion in those days came from church ceremonies, prayers the priests told them to recite, or money the priests collected for things like forgiving sins and baptizing little babies. The true new birth that Jesus told Nicodemus about was almost forgotten.

Ulrich's friends shared with him the things they found in the Bible. They shared things like baptizing grown-ups once they believed in Jesus instead of when they were babies. But Ulrich

Joining the Anabaptists was a serious decision;
one that nobody made lightly

didn't want to lose the support of the state by teaching things the local officials wouldn't agree with. He did not listen to what they said.

His plan was to take the church back to the way it had been in Constantine's time, instead of the days of the Apostles. His friends began to meet in secret in each other's homes to study God's Word. They were so touched by what they learned that even the threat of death didn't stop them. Soon they agreed to baptize each other the way Jesus taught.

Everywhere these men went they shared what they had found. Their message of God's love and obedience to Him spread like wildfire across the countryside. People were eager to know more about God.

The leaders of the country saw that many people joined this group and they were afraid their whole way of life would fall apart if the church and the government were separated like these men were teaching. The officials quickly made laws to punish anyone who became part of this new church. Still more people gathered to hear the wonderful new message of hope.

Many of the Anabaptist's secret meetings were held in caves in the mountains

The authorities called these people Anabaptists, meaning to baptize again. As their numbers grew, the punishments got worse and worse. They were fined and thrown into prison. They were tortured too horribly to imagine. Many were finally killed. All through these things the Anabaptists loved their enemies and did not fight back. This was a new idea, and the Swiss army saw that they would not have enough soldiers if too many men joined the Anabaptists. The persecution grew stronger and even more terrible.

The non-resistant Anabaptists would not join the Swiss Army

Hundreds of Anabaptists were put in prison or killed. Still their churches grew. The harder the rulers tried to get rid of them, the more there were! In Switzerland, Germany, Holland, and Austria the Anabaptists thrived in spite of the persecution. They had to meet late at night so they could avoid the dreaded "Taufer-Jager." These were men that had been hired to hunt the Anabaptists and turn them in to the authorities.

Sometimes the meeting places were rocky caves on the mountainsides or little huts high up in the Alps. Many barns and houses even had little hiding places where Anabaptist leaders could hide if they were being chased. Sometimes they were trapped in these cramped little hideouts for several days.

Many of the Anabaptist services were held in
little huts high up in the rocky Alps

The Anabaptists were respected for their godly actions and high ideals, even by friends and neighbors who had not joined them. Because of this, the officials had a hard time finding men who would betray them. Often they ended up hiring criminals as Taufer-Jagers. Fresh out of prison, these men had no respect for the peaceful Anabaptists and treated them in terrible ways. Still, the Anabaptists would not fight back.

The Anabaptist-hunters kept watch for the people on their
lists in the town marketplaces and the countryside

The Anabaptists turned the other cheek and tried to live as Jesus taught. Because of this, they were imprisoned, tortured, and killed. They suffered the loss of family, friends, their homes, and sometimes all they had. Many of them left all they knew and fled to America on slow, disease-filled ships. Often families had to bury loved ones at sea, and arrived in their new homes penniless. Do we love God and His Word so much that we would give all we have, even our lives, to win the Crown of Life?

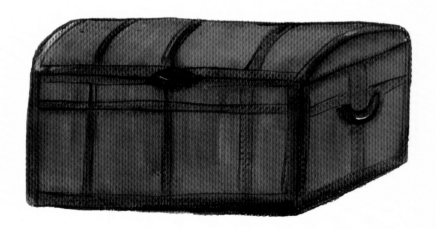

The Anabaptists took with them what they could
and left the rest when fleeing to America